To

_____

From

_____

Date

_____

God and Me!

and

FOR LITTLE ONES

My First Devotional for Toddler Girls

Ages 2-3

ROSEKiDZ

God and Me!® For Little Ones©2016 Rose Publishing, All rights reserved.

Published by Rose Kidz®
an imprint of Hendrickson Publishing Group
Rose Publishing, LLC
P.O. Box 3473
Peabody, Massachusetts 01961-3473 USA
www.hendricksonpublishinggroup.com
All rights reserved.

Cover and interior design by Mary pat Pino
Illustrated by Olga and Aleksey Ivanov
Written by Mary Gross Davis
Contributing Editor: Cashmere Walker

ISBN: 978-1-58411-182-5
RoseKidz® reorder number L46841
JUVENILE NONFICTION/Religious/Christian/Devotional & Prayer

Printed in China
Printed June 2020

"To all children of God"

O. & A. I.

It's Good to Be Kind

When Emma's mommy came home from the hospital, she held Emma's baby sister, Mia.

"Yay!" Emma squealed excitedly, "I'm a big girl. I'm a big sister!"

But, soon it was hard to be nice to the baby. Baby Mia was cranky. She grabbed Emma's toys. She slobbered on Emma's favorite teddy bear.

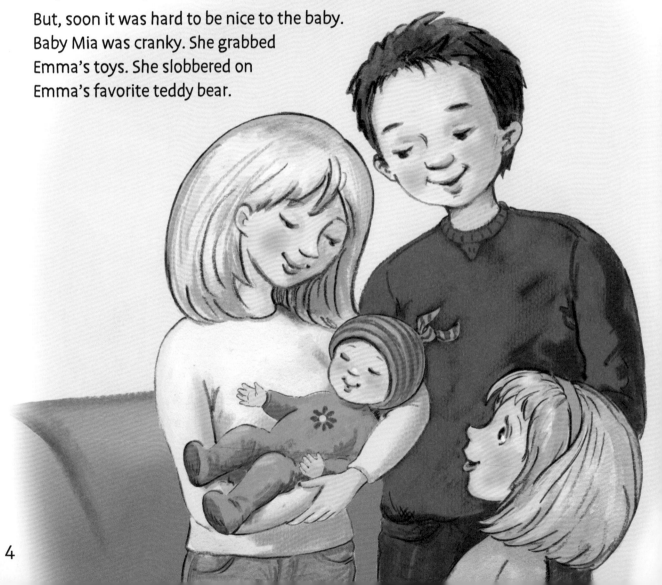

Sometimes Emma wanted to be mean. Sometimes she wanted to scream, "Don't touch that; it's mine!"

But Emma chose to be nice. She let Mia hold her toys. She didn't yell at the baby and helped mommy rock her back and forth to sleep.

"Emma, thank you for being kind to Mia. It makes you happy. It makes me happy. And it makes God happy, too!" Mommy said.

Talk about It

What could Emma do that Mia could not do?

What did Emma do to be kind to her sister?

What is a way you are kind to someone in your family?

Try This!

Play this game together. Ask, "When it is morning, what's a way you can be kind?" Tell or act out a way. Then ask and tell about ways to be kind at other times (lunch time, night time, bath time, etc.).

Parents, you can answer, too!

Prayer

God, thank you for being kind
to us. Please help us to be kind.
We know it makes you happy.
It makes us happy, too!
In Jesus' name, amen.

God's Words
Be kind. (See Ephesians 4:32.)

It's Good to Obey

"It's time for your nap," Mommy told Emily, "please go lie down."

But Emily didn't want to lie down. She ran to the backyard and played in the sandbox instead. As Emily played, Mommy found her.

"Emily, you didn't obey me," she said sadly. "I wanted you to nap because Grandma and Grandpa are visiting tonight. Now you might have to go to bed early and miss the fun."

Emily felt sad, too. She brushed off the sand and said, "I'm sorry, Mommy. I'll nap now."

Emily lay down and prayed, "God, I'm saying 'sorry' to you, too. Please help me to obey Mommy."

Emily felt better and napped. Then she stayed up and played with Grandma and Grandpa!

Talk about It

What did Mommy tell Emily to do? What did Emily do instead?

Who did she say "sorry" to?

When are times you obey your parents?

How do you feel when you obey your mom or dad?

Try This!

Play an "obey" game with your family. Have Mom or Dad give directions like, "Touch your head. Now touch your toes. Turn around." After everyone has obeyed say, "Yay! Yay! We DID obey!"

Dear Jesus, thank you for loving me all the time. I am sorry for times I disobey. Please help me obey my mom and dad.

In Jesus' name, amen.

God's Words
Children, obey your parents. (See Ephesians 6:1.)

11

It's Good to be Thankful

Charlotte and her daddy liked playing a game while walking.

"Find something red that we can thank God for," Daddy said.

Charlotte looked everywhere. She saw a pretty pot of red flowers and saw a fire truck ZOOM past them.

"There's LOTS of red!" Charlotte laughed. "Thank you, God, for the pretty red flowers. Thank you, God, for BIG red fire trucks. And thank you, God, for my red jacket. It keeps me warm!"

"Your turn, Daddy!" said Charlotte. "Find something GREEN."

Daddy said, "Oh, wow! Thank you, God, for green leaves. Thank you, God, for my green shoes. Thank you, God, for my green girl, Charlotte! I love her!"

Charlotte laughed. "Silly Daddy! I'm not GREEN!"

"No, you are not," Daddy agreed, "but I am thankful you're my daughter!"

Talk about It

What game did Charlotte and her daddy play?

Who made red things? Green things? Who made you?

Look around. What is something you can thank God for right now?

Try This!

Look back at the picture of Charlotte and her daddy. What are some blue things you could thank God for? Some orange things? Name each one, and then say, "Thank you, God!"

God, you are good. Thank you for the good things you give me. Thank you for loving me! In Jesus' name, amen.

God's Words
Give thanks to the Lord. (See 1 Thessalonians 5:18.)

It Is Good to Trust God

Ava loved playing in her backyard.

But every day, the dog next door RAN to the fence and BARKED.

He scared her!

Ava rushed inside.

"What's wrong?" Mother asked.

"The DOG!" cried Ava. "He's mean and LOUD!"

Mother said, "His name is Jake. He's a nice dog. Let's ask God to help us be brave."

Mother prayed, which made Ava feel better.

"Let's go meet Jake," Mother suggested.

After her mother asked the neighbor, they went into their neighbor's backyard. Ava felt scared, but she knew God would help her.

There was that DOG. Ava held out her hand. Jake sniffed and licked her!

"I'm not scared," she laughed. "Now we're friends!"

"Thank you, God, for helping us!" Mother said.

Talk about It

What is something that scares you?

Who is always with us? Who will help us?

When can we pray to God?

Try This!

Draw a picture of something that makes you feel scared. Show it to an adult. Together, talk about the picture and ask God for help!

God, thank You for always being with me. Please help me remember to talk to you when I am scared. In Jesus' name, amen.

God's Words

Do not be afraid. I will help you. (See Isaiah 41:13.)

It's Good to Share

"It's MINE!" Sophia shouted at Olivia.

Miss Brenda walked over. She said, "Girls, we can share. Sophia, it's your turn with the doll. Then it's Olivia's turn."

While Sophia played, Miss Brenda pulled out a NEW doll. She gave it to Olivia to play with.

"Whose doll is THAT?" Sophia asked Miss Brenda.

"Right now, it's Olivia's doll," Miss Brenda replied.

"It's MY turn to have Olivia's doll!" Sophia exclaimed.

"I'll tell you when it's your turn," Miss Brenda said.

After a minute, Miss Brenda said, "It's time to trade."

Olivia and Sophia traded back and forth. Then they played with the dolls together!

"Sharing is what God's Word says to do," smiled Miss Brenda. "I am happy to see you sharing!"

Talk about It

When has someone shared with you?

What toys do you like to play with?

Who can you take turns with?

Try This!

Play this game with someone in your family. Sit on the floor across from each other. Roll a ball back and forth. Say this rhyme as you play:

> I roll the ball to you;
> You roll the ball to me.
> We take turns to share the ball.
> We're glad to share, you see!

Dear God, I love you. Please help me to take turns. Please help me to share. I want to make you glad. In Jesus' name, amen.

God's Words
Do good and share. (See Hebrews 13:16.)

Mommy and Abigail were out in the backyard when they heard Miss Willa calling her cat, Leo.

"Leo! Where ARE you?" Miss Willa shouted.

"Let's see if we can help Miss Willa," said Mommy.

They talked to the man next door. Then they talked to Abigail's big brother, Jaydon. "Don't worry. We will find him," Jaydon assured them.

They ran up the street. They searched in trees and under bushes. No Leo!

They walked down another street and heard a MEOW! Abigail peered under a porch.

"Leo's stuck!" she shouted.

Jaydon crawled under the porch, pulled Leo out and carried him home.

"Thank you for helping me!" Miss Willa exclaimed.

Jaydon told Abigail, "I'm happy we helped Miss Willa and Leo. God put us next door to help them!"

Talk about It

Who is a person who has helped you? How did the person help?

What is one way you help in your family?

How can you help a person in your neighborhood?

Try This!

Look at the picture below. Look for ways people are helping each other. How many ways can you count?

Prayer

Dear God, thank you for people we can help. It makes us feel happy to help them. In Jesus' name, amen.

God's Words
Help your neighbor. (See Romans 15:2.)

27

It's Good to Show Love

Madison played with Isabella in the sandbox at the park. Suddenly a new boy ran up to the sandbox. Madison didn't know him. She felt nervous, but she knew God wanted her to show love.

"Come build a sand mountain with us!" she called to him. He smiled and joined them.

"My name's Kamil," he said.

"My name's Madison," she replied, "I like building hills in the sand."

"Me, too!" agreed Kamil, "I like how SQUISHY the sand feels!"

"Me too!" giggled Madison.

When it was time for Kamil to leave with his mom, he waved to the girls and said, "Bye, friends!"

Madison told Isabella, "I like Kamil. He's no longer the new boy, he's our friend!"

Talk about It

Think of a friend. What are ways you are like your friend?

What are ways you are different from your friend?

What are ways you can show love?

Try This!

Play a game in your family. How many people have the same color eyes? The same color hair? How many people have straight hair? Curly hair? Whose favorite food is the same?

Dear Jesus, thank you for new friends. Please help me show love to everyone! In Jesus' name, amen.

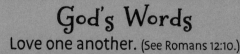

God's Words
Love one another. (See Romans 12:10.)

32